# minedition

North American edition published 2014 by Michael Neugebauer Publishing Ltd. Hong Kong

Michael Neugebauer Publishing Ltd., Unit 23, 7F, Kowloon Industrial Centre
15 Wang Hoi Road, Kowloon, Hong Kong. Phone +852 2807 1711,
e-mail: info@minedition.com
This book was printed in September 2014 at L.Rex Ltd 3/F., Blue Box Factory Building,
25 Hing Wo Street, Tin Wan, Aberdeen, Hong Kong, China
Typesetting in Clearface by Morris Fuller Benton
Color separations from slides and negatives by Pixelstorm, Vienna.
Library of Congress Cataloging-in-Publication Data available upon request.

ISBN 978-988-8240-83-8

10 9 8 7 6 5 4 3 2 1
First impression

For more information please visit our website: **www.minedition.com**
For more photos of Jane Goodall and her chimpanzees, visit: **www.minephoto.com**

# Jane Goodall
# The Chimpanzee Children of Gombe

Photos by Michael Neugebauer

## 50 YEARS WITH JANE GOODALL AT GOMBE NATIONAL PARK

I began studying the chimpanzees of Gombe National Park, in Tanzania, way back in 1960. At the beginning I was usually alone in the forest. The chimpanzees were shy and ran off whenever they saw me. But at last they got used to me, and to the students and field staff who came to help collect information.

The community we studied has always had about fifty individuals. And every chimpanzee has his or her own personality – just like us. In fact, they are like us in so many ways. They can be violent and aggressive, but mostly they are peaceful, and if they do fight they usually make up quickly.

Now I would like you to come with me into the forest. We will pretend it's just one day but actually we shall be going back every few years so that we can find out what happens with the different families.

If we spot chimps in the distance we shall have to use binoculars to see what is going on. Aha! It's a mother and her family feasting on tasty leaf buds. The forest provides the animals who live here with so many different kinds of food – fruit, leaves, flowers, seeds, and stems. Chimpanzees also eat insects. And sometimes they hunt for meat. We may find bigger groups – if a delicious fruit that has just ripened on one tree for example. And sometimes they travel alone.

When friendly chimpanzees meet they often kiss, just like we do. Fifi's infant Ferdinand is trying to reach Gremlin to give her a kiss as well.

Let me introduce you to some very special chimps - the F-family and the G-family.
Left to right: in front, Ferdinand, Gaia and Galahad; behind, Gremlin, Fifi and Faustino. They spend a lot of time together and their children are great playmates.
These are just two of the five families at Gombe with two or more young children. They are the two I know best. Sons and daughters spend a lot of time with their mothers even when they are quite grown up. They can live to be 60 years or more.

This is one of Fifi's children with her first baby.
I always love watching mothers and their families. In chimp society there are good mothers and not so good mothers.
It is the same for us – and I was lucky. I had a wonderful mother.

For the first three months of their lives, chimp babies are always clinging to their mother's hair. Right from the start they can hold on tight with their strong little fingers. At first they cling on underneath when the mother is travelling. When they are about five months old they start riding on her back. And they start to walk – just a few steps – at about the same time.

We all fell in love with Gremlin's infant son, Galahad — including Gremlin herself! Just look at his happy play face as he practices climbing. He begins to do acrobatics — but still he keeps close to his mother. And she spends a lot of time playing with him.

If you have ever climbed trees – I did when I was a child – you know it's easier to climb up than down. Kittens are always getting stuck in trees. Luckily for Galahad, when he gets into a difficult place, Gremlin is quick to reach down and rescue him. She is a really good mother.

When you were little you were fed foods that were good for you. Chimpanzee infants learn what to eat by tasting the food in their mothers' mouths. They also learn by watching what adults do and then imitating what they see. This is how they learn to use stems to fish for termites. And they learn about the other ways that chimps of their community use different objects as tools – like sticks and rocks and leaves.

If we listen carefully we shall hear Ferdinand softly whimpering. He is trying to persuade mother Fifi to move on. "Mom, I want to go." Finally she gives in – but she looks tired, don't you think? Probably she thinks her 5 year–old son is really too big to ride on her back. And she is already pregnant with her next baby.

It is always exciting when a new baby arrives – it doesn't happen that often because there is usually a five-year span between births. You can see that Fifi and her daughter Flossie are fascinated by Fanni's brand new baby, Fax.

Later Flossi will be allowed to groom, play with and finally carry her little nephew. All this will be really useful when she has her own first baby.

I absolutely love to watch chimpanzee youngsters playing together. They are having such fun, dangling, laughing and chasing each other...

Round and round a tree.
Round and round Mom.
Wouldn't you like to join in!

And when the mother is traveling on her own and there are no other chimp infants to play with, there are always toys in the forest. See the dry gourd Faustino has found? It has some seeds in it and he is shaking it just like a baby's rattle!

There are many troops of baboons at Gombe and sometimes young chimps and young baboons play together.

And you can see here that Gaia and Hector have become really good friends.

We've been studying Gombe's baboons for almost 50 years. Unlike the chimps, they spend a lot of time down on the beach of Lake Tanganyika.

You can never get bored watching a baboon troop because there is always something going on – playing, fighting, grooming or just resting in the sun.

When my son, nicknamed Grub, was small he played with the children of the Tanzanian staff. And when I watched them I could see how they behaved so much like the chimpanzee children I knew so well. In fact chimpanzees are more like us than any other living creature. They love and care for each other, squabble and make it up with hugging, and beg for food with outstretched hand. They laugh and cry (though they don't have tears). And they have emotions like happiness, sadness, fear, anger and so on. And of course they feel pain.

I'm sure you know that lots of other animals have emotions similar to ours – including our dogs and cats.

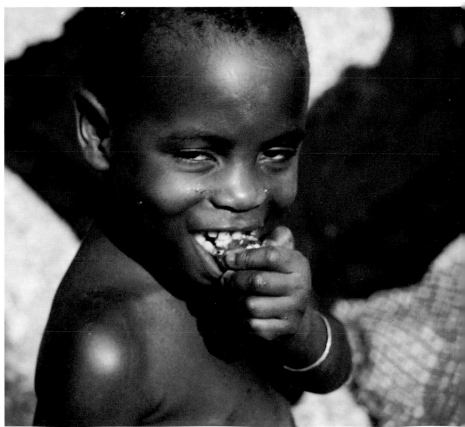

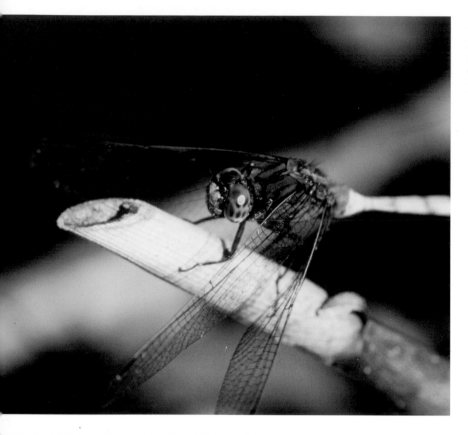

When we are walking in Gombe there will be days when we do not find chimps.
But even if they are not around, we will certainly find interesting things to look at and learn about.

I learned to identify countless fascinating birds – like this little grass finch. Some of them have brilliant colours, many have beautiful songs.

And here is a skink, a kind of lizard. At different times of year we shall find different flowers – especially in the rainy season.
And there are so many insects. See the beautiful dragonfly and lovely moth.

And, of course, there are lots of butterflies.
By the way, don't you think it should be
"flutter by?"
After all, that's what they do – they flutter
past you. Anyway, that's what I call them!

If we could spend longer in the forest I could introduce you to some of the other animals that I have got to know so well. There are the beautiful bushbucks. And I specially love the bushpigs – they are very fierce when they are protecting their babies. There is the huge rather mysterious Verrauxs Eagle Owl – I've only ever seen one, but you hear the call at night. There are very many snakes but you don't often see them unless you are looking for them. And then there are four different species of monkey – five if you count baboons.

Today we are lucky – for here is a red colobus, my very favorite monkey.
They live in big troops and they have special pathways through the forest. There is one path for the grown up monkeys – they have to take huge leaps from one tree to the next. And then there is a path for the juveniles who can't jump as far.

The waterfall in Kakombe Valley is the most spiritual place for me. And the spray makes it beautifully cool even on the hottest day. We can stop here and listen to the music of the falling water. And I can tell you about the medicine men who used to come here for special ceremonies before Gombe was a protected area.

How lucky. Now I can introduce you to Gremlin and her twin daughters, Golden and Glitta. It is not often that a chimpanzee gives birth to twins. In 50 years we have only seen this four times, and so far Gremlin is the only one who has successfully managed to raise both. It is very difficult to look after two babies at the same time in the wild. Just think about having two small infants clinging to your belly. And Gremlin had to produce twice as much milk.

Golden and Glitta, are not at all alike. Glitta is more adventurous, Golden is always wanting to be close to Mom. Gaia is absolutely fascinated – I think she grooms her mother? Gremlin so much just to stay close to the twins.

Now, what on earth is happening here? Gremlin's oldest son Galahad has found an umbrella, used by a film team to protect their equipment from the rain. Adventurous Glitta is the first to notice.

But soon the whole family gathers round to investigate. And look, Glitta has already learned to ride on her mother's back.

As they get older, the twins do lots of things together. And they love playing with their elder brother and sister. Golden prefers to play with Gaia who is more gentle than her brother. But Glitta loves a rough and tumble with big brother Galahad.

See how Glitta grabs onto overhead branches during travel. Its very irritating for her mother, who has to keep stopping. And Gaia seems a bit worried when the infant wants to swing off on a vine. She is a real help to her mother, always watching out for one or other of the twins. What a wonderful family.

Whatever is that little guy doing up there? You've probably noticed that chimp children can use their feet as extra hands. That's why they are so good at climbing.

I think we are all getting a bit weary after our day in the forest. The chimps have been feeding, playing and grooming, and now it's evening and they are looking for places to sleep.

We must be very quiet – Shhh!
And ah! See up there, high in the trees
Ferdinand has bent over lots of branches to
make a comfortable leafy nest. Faustino is
watching. Soon he will know how to make his
own bed, but for the time being she will go and
curl up with her mother.
And now, with the sun setting over the lake, we
must go back and have our own supper. And
when you lie cosy in your bed, think about the
chimps, and all you have learned. Thank you for
coming with me. We've had a great time at
Gombe together, haven't we?

*Plight of Chimpanzees in the Wild*

*Chimpanzees are only found (in the wild) in Africa. Once there were more than a million. Today there are no more than 300,000, probably less in the forests of 21 countries. The largest populations are in the Congo Basin.*

*Why are they disappearing? Because they are losing their habitat. Foreign logging companies are greedy for the wealth represented by the beautiful trees. Local human populations are growing and cutting down more and more forest – to sell the wood, to make charcoal, or to make space for new villages, for grazing cattle and so on. And because logging, mining and oil and gas companies are creating roads deep into the forest, hunters can reach places that were inaccessible before.*

*The bushmeat trade is the commercial killing of animals for food – not for hungry villagers but for the city people who pay more for meat from the forest. Any animals are killed, from elephants to birds and bats. Including chimpanzees and gorillas and monkeys.*

*Sanctuaries*

*Often, when I watch the chimpanzee children with their mothers, brothers and sisters and friends, playing and grooming in the forest, I think of all the others, who are not so lucky. This infant was born in the wild. His mother loved him and protected him. But then she was shot (for food) and his life changed forever.*

*There are hundreds of orphans like him. Hunters try to sell them in the markets. Because chimpanzees are an endangered species, killing and selling them is illegal. So the government will confiscate them. Then what happens?*

Organizations like the Jane Goodall Institute try to rescue and care for as many as possible to provide new homes and friends in sanctuaries. The biggest of these, Tchimpounga, is in the Republic of Congo where we are caring for more than 150. Many of them are now grown up. Luckily the government has given us three beautiful islands on the Kouilou River and already some of the chimpanzees are living there.

There is a lot of room on the islands, which are covered with tropical forest. But we still have to provide some of their food. They have a dormitory where they can sleep if they choose and where they can be cared for if they are sick.

It costs JGI a lot of money to care for all these chimpanzees, and we would love you to help with a donation, or by becoming a "Chimp Guardian."

For details about the programme in your country check *www.janegoodall.org*

## THE JANE GOODALL INSTITUTE (JGI)

*Only if we understand can we care*
*Only if we care will we help*
*Only if we help shall all be saved*

*In 1977 the first JGI was incorporated as a not for profit organization. Funds raised, through my lectures and donations from members, enabled me to continue the research at Gombe. From the start the mission of JGI was broad: to conduct chimpanzee research in the wild and in captivity, to improve conditions for chimpanzees in captive situations, to work to conserve chimpanzees and their habitats, and to create and conduct programs to empower and educate young people.*
*One of our most important programs is TACARE (TAKE CARE). It was initiated in 1994 to improve the lives of the people (in ways they wanted) living in 12 villages around Gombe national park. It now operates in 52 villages, and similar programs operate in Uganda, Democratic Republic of Congo, Republic of Congo and Senegal.*

## ROOTS & SHOOTS

*Every individual matters*
*Every individual has a role to play*
*Every individual makes a difference – every day.*

*Roots & Shoots began in 1991 with 12 Tanzanian High School Students who met on my veranda to discuss things that bothered them. And I persuaded them that they themselves could do something about their concerns.*
*Each group chooses for itself three projects that will make the world around them a better place. One to help humans, one for other animals, one for the environment. Such as visiting the elderly; helping out at an animal shelter (or becoming a chimp guardian!); clearing litter or planting trees - whatever they feel is appropriate for their local area.*

*Today there are R&S groups in more than 135 countries, with members from pre-school through university, and increasing numbers of adults forming groups. We reckon there are about 150,000 groups around the world. The collective impact is huge.*
*And, most importantly, members are empowered, ready to tackle the problems of their world.*